Celebrating Christ in History:
Reformation Day

Hal and Melanie Young

Great Waters Press
Making Biblical Family Life Practical

Celebrating Christ in History: Reformation Day

©2017 by Hal & Melanie Young, All Rights Reserved
Great Waters Press
www.GreatWatersPress.com

If purchased in eBook format, this eBook is not licensed for resale. This license is personal to the original purchaser and may not be sold, loaned, or otherwise transferred to third parties or additional users. Purchaser may make one copy for each member of their immediate household. Additional Licenses should be purchased if you'd like to share this eBook with anyone outside your family. Unlimited copies may be made only of pages containing words of hymns or recipes.

Contact info@greatwaterspress.com for information.

Copying for school or co-op use is strictly prohibited. Each student should purchase their own copy.

No part of this publication may otherwise be published, reproduced, stored in a retrieval system, or transmitted or copied in any form or by any means now known or hereafter developed, whether electronic, mechanical, or otherwise, without prior written permission of the publisher. Illegal use, copying, publication, transfer or distribution is considered copyright infringement according to Sections 107 and 108 and other relevant portions of the United States Copyright Act.

The use of any trademarked names does not imply endorsement or approval by the companies holding those trademarks. This document is intended only to enhance your user experience.

Cover Design by Melanie Young, ©2017.

Unless otherwise indicated, Scripture references are from the New King James Version. Copyright © 1982 by Thomas Nelson, Inc. Or, from the ESV® Bible (The Holy Bible, English Standard Version®), copyright © 2001 by Crossway, a publishing ministry of Good News Publishers. Both used by permission. All rights reserved.

Table of Contents

What is Reformation Day? 5
Why Remember Church History? 7
After the Apostles 8
Early Reformers Suffered 10
The Beginning of the Reformation 12
The Problem of Indulgences 14
Luther's Final Break with Rome 17
The Bible in the Common Language 20
A Final Note 21
The Five Solas of the Reformation 23
The Spread of the Reformation 25
Unfinished Business, or, "Semper Reformanda" 26
The Apostle's Creed 29
The Nicene Creed 30
How Can We Celebrate? 31
Wittenberg Door Pattern 34
"The Battle Hymn of the Reformation" 35
A Mighty Fortress 38
All People That On Earth Do Dwell: "Old One Hundredth" 39
Now Thank We All Our God 40
Who Puts His Trust in God Most Just 41
Reformation Day Feast 42
    Bratwurst with Sauerkraut 44
    Hot German Potato Salad 46
    Himmel und Erde 47
    Grandma's Green Beans 49

Cheese Fondue 50

Raclette 52

Fondue Bourguignonne 54

Marchand du Vin Sauce 56

Roasted Asparagus 57

Instant Pot™ Apple Sauce 58

What About the Other Holiday? 59

What is Reformation Day?

Are you as surprised as we were to find out that Reformation Day has been celebrated as a holiday in the church since at least 1567? We were delighted to find out that we could enjoy a holiday to remember true heroism — those who faced death and thereby opened the door for many to find eternal life!

Over the hundreds of years since the New Testament was written, the church drifted further and further from the Word of God. Occasionally, someone would rise up and try to draw people back to the gospel, but either their teachings didn't spread widely or they were martyred before they could. In the 1500's, though, the Lord raised up a leader who changed the course of history – a German priest and theologian named Martin Luther.

Martin Luther
(Workshop of Lucas Cranach the Elder, 1532)

On October 31, 1517, he nailed a notice to the door of the church, a common practice itself since the broad heavy doors were routinely used as bulletin boards. He chose the Eve of All Saint's Day to post the theses because the next day was a festival which would see the church full of the scholars he wanted to discuss these things with.

The timing was providential. Less than a century before, Gutenberg had invented the printing press, and by the time of Luther's act, there were hundreds of presses across Europe. Luther's challenge was soon printed and the list of propositions known as "The 95 Theses" lit a firestorm of controversy that quickly spread across Germany and central Europe.

Luther had attracted the attention not only of academics and churchmen like himself, but the wrath of Pope Leo X and the Holy Roman Emperor, Charles V, as well!

By the fiftieth anniversary of the posting of the Ninety-Five Theses in 1567, churches were celebrating Reformation Day as a way to remember what God had done. That means that Reformation Day has been celebrated for four hundred and fifty years! Let's talk about the history of the Reformation, how we can celebrate it, and how to interact with the world about this.

Why Remember Church History?

Hal's pastor in college majored in church history, and occasionally remarked that understanding how God had guided His people through the centuries helped keep His people from stumbling today. "It is useful to know that the really nifty insight that occurred to you during your morning devotions was actually condemned by the entire church in the Fifth Century," he said.

It's clear from the Bible that God wants us to remember and talk about His marvelous work throughout history. He established the Jewish feasts as memorials to His delivering the Jews from bondage, and parents are told to teach their kids why holidays and monuments exist (Exodus 12:26, Deuteronomy 32:7, and Psalm 78:3-6 for just a few examples). Jesus commanded the disciples to observe the Lord's Supper *"in remembrance of Me"* (Luke 22:19), the book of Hebrews records the faith of early believers and martyrs (chapter 11), and Paul points to Israel's history and says, *"these things happened to them as examples, and they were written for our admonition ..."* (1 Corinthians 10:11)

> *Great is the Lord, and greatly to be praised ...*
> *One generation shall praise Your works to another,*
> *And shall declare Your mighty acts.* (Psalm 145:3-4)

God's work in history didn't end with the ancient nation of Israel, and His work with the church didn't stop when the Bible was completed at the end of the First Century. Even while the Bible was still being recorded, the church was wrestling with fundamental questions about God, man, and the faith – for example, does the gospel extend to Gentiles as well as Jews? Do Gentiles have to adopt Jewish laws to please God? If Christ fulfilled the Law, what do we do with it now?

The apostles, with the guidance of the Holy Spirit, discovered the connection between the recorded words of the Bible and their current questions. Over and over, we see that those who had the Word had often misunderstood what God intended, or else had lost their focus on His teaching and substituted their own ideas for God's. Often the answers were "hidden in plain sight" – but without the Spirit, their understanding was clouded or even blind. Much of the apostles' writing from Romans to Revelation has the echo of "Aha!" in the background.

From the beginning, that has been the history of the Christian church.

Paul preaching in Athens (Illustration from The New Testament, Hewett & Spooner Publishers, 1850)

AFTER THE APOSTLES

For many years after the time of the Apostles – in fact, even during their lifetimes! – the church was wrestling to understand the Bible's teaching about the Messiah. Was Jesus human? Was He divine? Or was He somehow both at the same time? (The last is the right answer, by the way.)

By the time of St. Augustine, in the mid-400's, the church was settling down to a Biblical understanding of the nature of Christ. This is the time which gave us the Apostles' Creed and the Nicene Creed, which emphatically affirm Jesus in both His human flesh and His spiritual reality as well.

But a second question was moving to the front – the question of the jailer in Philippi, *"What must I do to be saved?"* (Acts 14:31)

During the years between the Apostles and the Middle Ages, the Roman Catholic Church was struggling with the implications of that question. What *is* the Gospel? Are we saved by faith alone, or is something else equally necessary? What role does the Church play in salvation? Can believers find answers in the Bible themselves, without the guidance of the Church?

At the same time, the Church was gaining more and more political power in Europe. The pope ruled significant territory in Italy and exercised tremendous influence over countries throughout Europe. For example, due to separate disputes between the kings of those countries and the Pope, the Church refused to conduct marriages or allow burial in sacred ground throughout England, France, and Norway. With promises of spiritual benefits, the papacy launched several massive military actions against the Muslim occupiers of the Holy Land. And from Pope Leo III's coronation of Charles the Great (Charlemagne) as "Emperor of the Romans," the Pope became a major player in the royal succession and policy of every Christian nation.

During this period, there were scholars and church leaders who questioned new developments in the Church's teaching and practice. Can believers approach God directly without the help of a priest? Can individual believers learn from the Bible themselves? Should worship services be the language of the people? Must believers learn Latin in order to read the Bible? Should church leaders live quiet, simple lives of service, or is it appropriate to reward their service with a luxurious or even royal lifestyle?

Early Reformers Suffered

Some of the earliest voices for reform led to monastic communities, following St. Benedict's call to come away from the temptations of the world and focus on simple, even ascetic, lifestyles of prayer, meditation, and service in celibate communities. Some of these became lasting institutions which did accomplish many things for the church and for western civilization.

But some who questioned the departure of church teaching from the Word of God fell into serious trouble. In the 12th Century a French layman named Peter Waldo questioned the growing wealth of the Church, taught that believers could approach God through Christ without a priest (a principle called "the priesthood of believers") and arranged for the first translation of the Bible into a modern European language. His ideas were declared heretical by two church councils and he and his followers, exiled from their homes, fled to the mountains to avoid further persecution.

John Wycliffe (Thomas Kirkby, 1828)

In the 14th Century, the English seminary professor John Wycliff taught similar principles and emphasized the Bible was the only sure guide to the faith and practice of the church. He assisted in the preparation of the first English Bible and had numerous conflicts with the papacy during his life. Though he died peacefully, a few years later the Church condemned him and his followers as heretics and had his bones dug up and burned.

Jan Hus at the Council of Konstanz (Karl Friedrich Lessing, 1842)

In the 15th Century, the Czech reformer Jan Hus preached against the Church's Crusades, the sale of indulgences, and moral failings among the clergy. He was an open admirer of Wycliff, whose work was rapidly being condemned, and eventually was arrested and accused of heresy himself. Although he called only for the council to convince him of error by using the Bible, Hus was condemned and burned at the stake. The horror which swept through the Czech nation led to actual warfare between the neighboring Catholic kingdoms and the Bohemian region which had adopted Hussite teachings.

The Beginning of the Reformation

In 1505, Martin Luther was a young German law student when he underwent a remarkable religious conversion. A near miss from a bolt of lightning seemed to be a warning from God, and in fear, he committed himself to becoming a monk. True to his word, Luther quickly wrapped up affairs at the university and presented himself as a candidate to the Augustinian monastery nearby.

Martin Luther as a Monk (Cranach, 1520)

He quickly progressed to the priesthood, but remained terrified and depressed over the state of his soul and his lack of peace before God. Luther did everything within his power to find forgiveness from God. He tried isolating himself in a religious community, hours of fasting and prayer, pilgrimage to holy shrines, veneration of saints and relics, and even self-flagellation (beating himself senseless to punish his body), but nothing gave him peace. A pilgrimage to Rome only disturbed his thoughts, as he watched the priests breezing through the most holy of ceremonies with no sign of reverence or the fear of God.

Luther's superiors thought to drive out his doubts and misery by pushing him into academic study and teaching. In a few years he completed his studies to be named a doctor of theology, and soon was recruited as a professor and pastor at the new University of Wittenberg in the principality of Saxony.

Wittenberg, Saxony (1536)

It was there that Luther discovered the key to his peace – the great truth that salvation comes by faith alone, not by completion of works of piety and penance. In the course of his studies in the book of Romans, Luther came across the verse, *"The just shall live by faith,"* in Romans 1:17. The emphasis on faith stunned him and he set out to learn more. His study led him to realize that all his efforts to earn the forgiveness of God through religious works was fruitless; indeed, the Bible told him that it is *"not by works of righteousness which we have done, but according to His mercy He saved us."* (Titus 3:5) Instead, salvation is the work of God, not of man at all; it comes to us as an undeserved, unearned blessing from the Father. *"For by grace you have been saved through faith, and that not of yourselves; it is the gift of God, not of works, lest anyone should boast."* (Ephesians 2:8-9)

Deepening his study in the Bible, Luther began to realize that many of the accepted practices and doctrines of the Church were not based on the Scripture but on later writing and decrees of men. Like Waldo, Wycliff, and Hus (as well as leaders within his own monastic order!), Luther began questioning these innovations – where does the Bible give worldly authority to the Pope? Does Christ require a human priest between sinners and Himself? Where is the Biblical example for Church leaders living like princes on the donations of poor believers? Why should the Church place human tradition above or alongside the Bible as authoritative?

The Problem of Indulgences

One issue which had been a problem in the Church for centuries was the sale of indulgences. The Church taught that Peter had been given the authority to forgive sins on earth, and that popes inherited that power, extending even to punishments beyond death.

An indulgence is a specific offer of forgiveness in response to acts of faith. These might be significant exercises of prayer and worship, travel on pilgrimages, participation in military crusades, or donations to charitable works.

This became a means of fundraising for the papacy, and for centuries reformers had pointed out it was corrupting the church. In some cases, it literally became an offer of forgiveness for money.

In 1514, Pope Leo X renewed an existing indulgence to raise funds for the re-building of St. Peter's Basilica in Rome. Under the terms of the proclamation, sponsors of the sale would receive half the amount collected. The newly-appointed Archbishop of Mainz, Albrecht of Brandenburg, was deeply in debt after purchasing his third church office from the pope, so beginning in 1519 he began promoting the indulgence with the help of a Dominican friar, Johann Tetzel, as his primary agent.

Pope Leo X (Raphael, c. 1517)

In his instructions to Tetzel, the archbishop reminded him that purchasers of this indulgence would receive "complete remission of all sins … and the punishment which one is obliged to undergo in Purgatory." Confession to a priest was normally required to receive such an indulgence, but in this case, "the intention of confessing at a suitable time" was sufficient. And even more, relatives who had already died could receive the same forgiveness, after a proper contribution had been made.[1]

Johann Tetzel (Source unknown, 1717)

The ruler of Saxony, the Elector Frederick the Wise, forbade Tetzel to enter his realm. Instead, the Dominican set up camp just across the river and maintained a brisk sale of the papal pardon to Saxons who came over, promising "As soon as a coin in the coffer rings, the soul from Purgatory springs."

Besides his job as professor, Luther was also the pastor of the castle church, and he was concerned about the number of his parishioners who were purchasing a document they believed guaranteed God would overlook their sins. Naturally, there is no mention of this practice in the Bible, since the forgiveness of sin is only by faith in the sacrifice of Christ. Since it was accepted Church doctrine, though, Luther wished to hold a thorough debate among his fellow professors and theologians about the practice. He framed the debate with a list of 95 propositions or theses concerning the sale of indulgences and other issues.

On October 31, 1517, the day before the Festival of All Saints[2], he posted his list on the heavy wooden door of the church – alongside other notices, for the church door was also used as a community bulletin board.

---

[1] From *Instructio Summaria ad Subcommissarios Poenitentiarum et Confessores* (W. Köhler, *Dokumente zum Ablassstreit*, pp. 104-16) as quoted in The Reformation, by Hans J. Hillerbrand, published by Harper & Row, publishers, Copyright 1964 by SCM Press Ltd and Harper and Row, Inc., Library of Congress catalog card number 64-15480, pp. 37-41.

[2] The English term was "All Hallows' Even" which gives us the contraction, Hallowe'en.

Luther Posts His 95 Theses (Ferdinand Pauwels, 1872)

From the beginning, Luther had no intention of dividing or leaving the Church of Rome, but the Ninety-Five Theses were a radical challenge to the Pope and many long-standing doctrines and practices. To his surprise, what Luther intended as an invitation to an academic controversy lit a fire across Germany.

Luther's theses, written in good academic Latin, were copied down and translated into German (apparently without his knowledge), then rapidly published through the new media of the day – Johannes Gutenberg's printing press (developed only a generation earlier). His call for a re-examination of the Church's teaching and policy struck a chord in many minds – some whose hearts responded to the idea for a simpler, heartfelt faith based on the Bible, and some who wished to see Rome's expansion and expense reigned in. And thanks to Gutenberg's invention, Luther's teaching spread faster and further than any earlier reformers such as Wycliff and Hus could have dreamed.

As Luther's ideas reached the community, he found sympathetic hearers and supporters growing around him. The rising tide of followers (and the change in the response to the indulgence) also attracted the attention of Pope Leo. He tried to reign in Luther with a series of debates against leading theologians, with no success. When Luther publicly proclaimed that the pope and church councils did not have exclusive authority to interpret the Bible, he was linked with the teaching of Jan Hus – and labeled a heretic.

In 1520, Pope Leo issued a papal bull (a formal decree) which gave Luther sixty days to retract nearly half of his 95 theses, or be excommunicated from the Church. In response, Luther publicly burned the document. The following month, he was dismissed from the Church.

Luther's Final Break with Rome

At that time, what we know as Germany was the Holy Roman Empire,[3] a collection of many small principalities like Saxony, each with its own prince or governing body, all of them answering to the young emperor Charles V. Because of the interconnections between the Church and earthly politics, Luther's conflict with Rome brought the civil authorities into a religious controversy.

The conflict had a political component as well. Many of the German states had begun to grumble against the expansion of the Church's wealth and influence in local affairs, believing that Rome and the Pope were meddling too much in worldly matters they felt were *their* responsibility. Some of the support or opposition to Luther's teaching was not religious at all!

Holy Roman Empire c. 1254
(*Historical Atlas,* William Shepherd, 1926)

---

[3] In fact, at this time it was called *Das Heiliges Römisches Reich Deutscher Nation* – the Holy Roman Empire of the German Nation. That title was dropped a few years before the empire dissolved in 1806.

Luther was commanded to appear before the Holy Roman Emperor, Charles V, in the city of Worms[4]. This was a meeting of the Diet, the legislative council of the Empire, bringing princes and rulers of the realm together with leaders of the church.

At the Diet of Worms, Luther was asked to confirm his authorship of a large number of books and pamphlets – which he did – and then ordered to recant. He protested that his writing covered so many topics, he could not withdraw all of them without denying many things that were not controversial to *anybody*. He begged for more time to consider his answer, and the Emperor grudgingly agreed to twenty-four hours. In the front of everybody's mind was the memory that the Czech reformer, Jan Hus, had made many of the same propositions decades earlier — and was burned at the stake in consequence.

Burning of Jan Hus at the Stake (Diebold Schilling the Older, Spiezer Chronik, *1485)*

---

[4] Pronounced "Vorms." This is important because the historic references to "The Diet of Worms" is too humorous otherwise.

Luther spent a sleepless night of anxious prayer. The next day, when he began to make a statement to the assembly, Luther was cut short and ordered to give a simple yes or no answer – would he recant, or not?

Full of the knowledge of what had happened to Hus in similar circumstances, Luther replied:

> *Since then Your Majesty and your lordships desire a simple reply, I will answer without horns and without teeth. Unless I am convinced by Scripture and plain reason–I do not accept the authority of popes and councils, for they have contradicted each other–my conscience is captive to the Word of God. I cannot and I will not recant anything, for to go against conscience is neither right nor safe.* **Here I stand. I cannot do otherwise. God help me. Amen.**

The Diet of Worms (Anton von Werner, 1877)

Luther stared death in the face and stood on the word of God in defiance of Pope and Emperor. The 21-year-old emperor was furious, but honored his guarantee of safe conduct and allowed Luther to return to Saxony. In the meantime, though, Charles declared Luther an outlaw, beyond legal protection, subject to

> *Confiscation and loss of body and belongings and all goods, fixed and movable, half of which will go to the Lord, and the other half to the accusers and denouncers. With other punishments as given more fully in the present edict and mandate.*

Wartburg Castle, Eisenach, Germany

The Bible in the Common Language

On his way home from Worms, Luther's supporters staged a mock kidnapping and hid the reformer in the Wartburg Castle near Eisenach. He spent eight months in hiding, writing a number of tracts and booklets, and most importantly, translating the New Testament from Greek to German. This not only gave the German people a readable version of the Bible for themselves, it helped establish a common language among the many German dialects. Luther's translation occupies the

Luther's study at Wartburg (c. 1900) – with the whalebone he used for a footstool

same place in German culture as the King James Version does in English, and in fact, inspired the early English translations by Miles Coverdale and through him, the Geneva Bible.

As religious conflicts and party factions erupted in Wittenberg and beyond, Luther came out of hiding and resumed open leadership of the new evangelical churches. Though he was still officially outlaw, the imperial edict was never enforced in German territory, and with the assistance of his trusted associate Philip Melanchthon, Luther was able to give shape to the growing Protestant movement. Besides his courageous stand for the authority of the Scriptures, Luther supervised the translation of the entire Bible into German, wrote many hymns and books, and created instructional catechisms for clergymen, families, and children. He followed his own teaching about the marriage of clergy, too, and married a former nun, Katherine von Bora; they had six children. Luther died in 1546 at the age of 62, in the town where he was born.

A Final Note

It should be added that while Luther was a faithful student of the Bible, a courageous defender of the truth found there, and a tireless servant of the churches he led, he was still a sinner saved by grace and a man of his own historical context.

Manners in the Middle Ages were more earthy than "polite" by our standards, and Luther said and wrote things with a saltiness of expression that can be both entertaining and shocking to modern readers.

Also, unexpected issues arose as Luther and the other reformers were sorting their way through the implications of a new understanding of Scripture. Luther had to deal with sects taking more radical positions than the Bible called for, including one led by a former colleague. He was forced to take sides in political disputes such as the Peasants' War, where he criticized both the workers and the nobility, but condoned the violence used to put down the uprising. He was pulled into a scandal when a prominent supporter took a second wife on the grounds that the Old Testament permitted it. And like most Europeans of his time, Luther agreed with and taught the anti-Semitic view that modern Jews inherited responsibility for the Crucifixion and should either convert or accept persecution.

Why should these be remembered? Simply to remind us that no human leader, no matter how heroic or important in history, is without his sins and shortcomings. Like Peter, Luther loved his Lord and followed Him closely, yet made bold and public mistakes that deserved the criticism he received.

On his deathbed, Luther was asked if he held fast to his faith in Christ and the doctrines he had taught; he said, very clearly, that he did. His last words rest on his understanding of man's deepest need of God's grace and forgiveness: "We are beggars: this is true."

Luther is buried in a simple tomb in the Castle Church of Wittenberg, just a few feet below the pulpit.

Pulpit and Luther's Tomb, Castle Church, Wittenberg, 1911 (Brück & Sohn, with permission)

The Five Solas of the Reformation

Many years after Luther, historians and theologians catalogued five basic principles which underlie the teaching of the Reformation. **They are referred to as "The Five Solas" from their Latin abbreviations** (Latin being the language of scholars and clergymen at that time). They emphasize the fundamental importance of each point.

Sola Scriptura – "Scripture Alone" – The reformers took their stand on the Bible as the bedrock source of Christian faith and practice. Luther's courageous defiance of the Emperor and the Pope reminded them that popes and church councils had frequently disagreed when proclaiming official doctrines, and only the Bible remains unchanging and secure. *"All Scripture is breathed out by God, that the man of God may be complete, equipped for every good work."* (2 Timothy 3:16)

Luther Monument (Frauenkirche, Dresden)

Sola Fide – "Faith Alone" – Luther found peace with God when he understood Romans 1:17, which says, *"The just shall live by faith,"* showing God as a loving father to His people and not an angry judge. When the Philippian jailer asked Paul *"What must I do to be saved?"* he was not given a list of religious exercises to complete or a course of hidden knowledge to understand. Paul told him simply, *"Believe in the Lord Jesus Christ, and you will be saved."* (Acts 16:31)

Sola Gratia – **"Grace Alone"** – Grace is the blessing of God which He gives without expecting us to earn it. We can never work our way to heaven; eternal life is a gift to undeserving sinners like ourselves. *"For you are saved by grace through faith, and that not of yourselves, it is a gift of God; not a result of works, lest any man should boast."* (Ephesians 2:8-9)

Solus Christus – **"Christ Alone"** – Salvation comes through the blood of Jesus Christ and the work of no one else. The prayers of saints or faithful acts of believers do nothing to bring forgiveness to the repentant sinner – pardon comes only through the sacrifice of God's Son. *"For there is no other name under heaven by which we must be saved."* (Acts 4:12)

Soli Deo Gloria – **"The Glory of God Alone"** – As faithful followers of the Lord, like Jesus we should be focused on the business of our heavenly Father. *"I am the LORD,"* He tells us in Isaiah 42:8, *"and My glory I will not give to another."* The apostle Paul tells us, *"Whatever you do, do all to the glory of God."* (1 Corinthians 10:31)

Luther's stand and his theology sparked the Protestant Reformation. Although the movement was originally intended to be a reformation of the Roman Catholic Church, when church authorities refused to change or even allow change, reformers reluctantly separated from the church and began to form new churches centered on the Word of God.

The Spread of the Reformation

Luther's reforms in Germany did not stay in Saxony. His courageous stand for the Biblical faith inspired other reformers across Europe. In the years after the Diet of Worms, Luther's doctrines spread to other parts of Germany, Scandinavia, and the Low Countries, while parallel movements sprang up in Switzerland, France, and Britain.

Other reformers developed slightly different understanding of certain doctrines. In Zurich, for example, the Swiss leader Ulrich Zwingli agreed with much of Luther's other teaching but debated his views on baptism and the Lord's Supper. A generation later in Geneva, the French-born reformer John Calvin established himself as the Reformation's leading theologian with his *Institutes of the Christian Religion,* but his followers also remained distinct from Luther's on several issues.

Calvin's Geneva became a safe haven for many leaders of the English Reformation. Although King Henry VIII of England initially defended the Catholic Church from Luther's criticisms, he turned against Rome when the pope refused him permission to divorce his first wife. Leaders in the English church who responded to Luther's teaching flourished for a time, but when Queen Mary came to the throne, they were brutally repressed. Some Protestant leaders were executed for their faith; others made their way to Geneva and continued their work among the English expatriate community. At the death of Queen Mary, her successor Elizabeth I ended the persecution and welcomed Reformed teaching back into England.

Sadly, competition between powerful monarchs with different religious convictions led to warfare across the Continent. Wars between the Reformed people of the Low Countries and their Catholic rulers were a major part of European politics for decades. Likewise, the shifting balance of political power between Catholic and Protestant parties in France led to persecution of the Reformed or Huguenot population there, many of whom immigrated to the new colonies in America. It was a sad period of history when Christians felt justified to mistreat or execute other Christians in the name of their particular theology.

Unfinished Business, *or*, "Semper Reformanda"

In 1674, a Dutch pastor named Jocodus van Lodenstein coined the phrase *Ecclesia Reformata, Semper Reformanda* – "the reformed church, always reforming." At that time, 150 years after Luther's break from Rome, the Protestant movement was well established and growing in many countries. Yet Van Lodenstein knew that we always need to be examining our lives and our beliefs to be sure we stay in step with the Bible and the Holy Spirit.

The rediscovery of salvation by grace through faith in Christ alone was a dramatic return to the principles of Scripture. Still, Luther and the other reformers found many other issues of church life remained to be discussed. Even today, five hundred years later, there are still differences between traditions in the Protestant churches:

What is the meaning of the Lord's Supper? The Church of Rome taught (and still teaches) that the physical bread and wine are changed in their substance by the ceremony of the Mass, becoming literally the body and blood of Christ when they are blessed by the priest. This is called *transubstantiation*.

The reformers believed this was unbiblical, but they disagreed on the proper understanding. Luther rejected *transubstantiation*, but taught that Jesus' body and blood joined with the bread and wine rather than replacing them; this is called *consubstantiation*.

The Swiss reformer Ulrich Zwingli taught that the bread and wine are symbolic only and simply remind us of Jesus' death. On the other hand, the French-Swiss reformer John Calvin taught that the physical elements of bread and wine are unchanged, but that Christ is spiritually present for believers through the action of the Holy Spirit.

Despite these differences, all the reformers agreed that the sacrament of the Lord's Supper (whether called by that name, Communion, or the Eucharist) should be a regular part of the believer's life and worship.

What about baptism? Protestants divided into two camps over who should receive baptism. The majority of early Protestants continued the practice of baptizing infant children of believing parents, teaching it was a sign of God's covenant similar to the Old Testament sign of circumcision. This is called *paedobaptism* (baptism of children).

Swiss reformer Ulrich Zwingli (Has Asper, 1531)

Others, beginning again with reformer Ulrich Zwingli, questioned this belief. Zwingli and those that came after taught that baptism was a sign of individual repentance and faith, and should only be given to believers who had professed faith in Christ for themselves (known as *credobaptism*, baptism of believers). Two branches of the church taught this: the Anabaptist movement (forerunners of the Amish, Mennonites, and Hutterites) and Baptists of the Reformed tradition (the English "Particular Baptists," and later the founders of the Southern Baptist Convention and several smaller Baptist denominations all adopted Calvin's theology).

Both positions can be argued from Scripture, and *have* been argued, since the time of Luther. Their agreement is that baptism does not actually change the believer, but is an act of obedience to Christ's command and example, a sign of faith in God's forgiveness and mercy, and a testimony to the world around us.

What is the relationship between believers, churches, and the state? Much of the strife which followed the Reformation came from a belief that the ruler had the right to specify the official religion of his realm. Interestingly enough, both Luther and the Pope would agree on this issue! The early Anabaptists were persecuted not because of their teaching on baptism, but because they taught that believers were called out of the business of the world, and therefore should not take oaths or military service.

Eventually even Protestant groups persecuted one another. The Church of England outlawed Presbyterian, Baptist, and Separatist pastors from preaching in the early 1600's, leading to the emigration of the Pilgrims. The Puritans who settled New England (themselves a minority group in the Church of England) forced the Baptist Roger Williams out of the Massachusetts Bay Colony. The American guarantee of freedom of religion, part of our founding Constitution, arose from these unhappy experiences!

THE APOSTLE'S CREED

Widely used since at least the 4th century, many phrases are from the New Testament.

I believe in God, the Father almighty,
    creator of heaven and earth.

I believe in Jesus Christ, his only Son, our Lord,
    who was conceived by the Holy Spirit
    and born of the virgin Mary.
    He suffered under Pontius Pilate,
    was crucified, died, and was buried;
    he descended to hell.
    The third day he rose again from the dead.
    He ascended to heaven
    and is seated at the right hand of God the Father almighty.
    From there he will come to judge the living and the dead.

I believe in the Holy Spirit,
    the holy catholic* church,
    the communion of saints,
    the forgiveness of sins,
    the resurrection of the body,
    and the life everlasting. Amen.

that is, church universal, all those who truly follow Christ

The Nicene Creed

Adopted by the Council of Nicea in 325 A.D. with additions by the Council of Constantinople in 381 A.D. and used by a wide variety of churches since as a basic statement of faith that we can all agree on.

We believe in one God,
    the Father almighty,
    maker of heaven and earth,
    of all things visible and invisible.
And in one Lord Jesus Christ,
    the only Son of God,
    begotten from the Father before all ages,
        God from God,
        Light from Light,
        true God from true God,
    begotten, not made;
    of the same essence as the Father.
    Through him all things were made.
    For us and for our salvation
        he came down from heaven;
        he became incarnate by the Holy Spirit and the virgin Mary,
        and was made human.
        He was crucified for us under Pontius Pilate;
        he suffered and was buried.
        The third day he rose again, according to the Scriptures.
        He ascended to heaven
        and is seated at the right hand of the Father.
        He will come again with glory
        to judge the living and the dead.
        His kingdom will never end.
And we believe in the Holy Spirit,
    the Lord, the giver of life.
    He proceeds from the Father and the Son,
    and with the Father and the Son is worshiped and glorified.
    He spoke through the prophets.
    We believe in one holy catholic and apostolic church.*
    We affirm one baptism for the forgiveness of sins.
    We look forward to the resurrection of the dead,
    and to life in the world to come. Amen.

*Refers to the church universal, that is, all those who truly follow Christ.

How Can We Celebrate?

Christians have been celebrating Reformation Day for nearly half a millennium. Over that long a period, as you can imagine, all kinds of celebrations have occurred. Although recognition of this day is not as common as it once was, it seems to be making a comeback.

One church we know of has a huge celebration which people attend in medieval costume. They have lectures on Reformation theology, but also a huge Renaissance- and Reformation-era faire with food, activities, and vendors. Activities like jousting tournaments (with foam tipped spears and hobby horses!), medieval games, calligraphy work, chain mail and wood-burning crafts, spits roasting joints, stew in bread bowls, simple printing crafts, foot races, and many other entertaining and educational pursuits could be included.

Sent's Reformation Party (Marianela Holmes, Used by Permission)

Our friends, Ed and Julia Sents of Iowa, sponsor a community Reformation Day celebration. Every year they choose a different reformer to focus on. They have someone teach about that Reformer and have entertainment appropriate for the time and country of that Reformer. The year they remembered the Scottish Reformer John Knox, for example, they invited a bagpiper!

They finish with a feast which is so looked forward to that once when we were in their area, during a trip to the store, we heard the cashier, a stranger, asking about the celebration and talk about how much she was looking forward to it. We love that they use this as an outreach to the community.

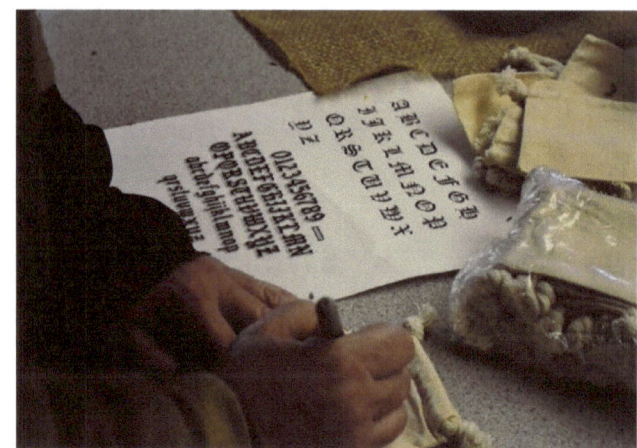
Sent's Reformation Party (Marianela Holmes, Used by Permission)

We attended another Reformation Day event at the home of Carl and Kim Trautman. Some attended in costume and others did not. They had games and activities that went along with the theme, some in a humorous way. The sauerbraten served was an old German family recipe of theirs.

We decided many years ago that Reformation Day was a tradition we wanted to perpetuate in our family. Holidays give us a time that's set aside to share history and truth with our children. What a great opportunity to teach our children the heroism of the fathers of our faith, and to talk about our sure foundation: Salvation is by grace through faith in the substitutionary death of the God-man Jesus Christ. That means that as God-made-flesh, He was infinite in nature and had no sins of his own to die for, so could die for the sins of all His people, taking the death they deserved on Himself. What a rich truth!

When we started doing this, we'd never been to any sort of Reformation Day event, so we made it up as we went along. We realized that distinctive foods and decorations gave us tastes and smells and sights that would engage our senses and help us remember the lessons of the day. Since the Reformation first took hold in Germany and Switzerland, we usually have a German or Swiss meal. Later in this book, we'll share some menus we've enjoyed and favorite recipes we've used at our table.

Since we've had young children at home for the past few decades (we have eight children, spanning nineteen years in age!), we've found that movies that tell the story are an enjoyable, profitable way to spend the evening. We've watched movies about Hus, Wycliffe, Calvin, and several about Martin Luther, but one has become such a favorite that our children demand it year after year. It's the old B&W *Martin Luther* film made in 1953 and starring Niall MacGinnis as the Reformer. A Lutheran organization sponsored the film and it is extremely true to history. The movie was even filmed at the actual location of some events and they did a good job finding actors who actually *looked* like Luther, Charles, and Pope Leo. The scene at Worms is classic! It's suitable for all ages, though our young children didn't like the first few minutes of introduction because it shows some rather alarming medieval art. Cover eyes for that minute or two and everyone will be fine. Go to our Reformation Day Resources page at www.RaisingRealMen.com/reformation for links to good movies.

Niall MacGinnis as Martin Luther (1953)

The movie is a little long, so be sure to start early enough in the evening for little ones to see the whole thing. Sometimes we serve the meal "dinner theatre" style to allow us more time.

During breaks we love to sing hymns of the Reformation. *A Mighty Fortress is Our God* was written by Martin Luther himself. *Now Thank We All Our God* and *We Gather Together* are connected with the Reformation too. All of which have very interesting stories we'll share in just a bit.

Our children do love our themed concession to the candy-intensive season **… we play "Pin the Theses on the Wittenberg Door."** We draw big fancy wooden doors on brown paper (we include a pattern to give you an idea how to do this) with a different treat written on each panel. We use Post-it™ notes for the Theses and play much as you play Pin the Tail on the Donkey. We blindfold each player and turn them around the number of years they are old (but cap it or the grown-ups would do nothing but spin!) Everybody wins something, which the boys actually don't mind as long as they get lots of candy!

Our friends are getting in to the spirit of things, too. One year, friends of ours came in the middle of the night and stuck a copy of the Theses on our door with a bag of candy and a sign, "You've been nailed!" Another set of friends had a bonfire "to burn the Papal Bull." However you celebrate…

Instead of justifying Christians participating in a holiday that is in no wise holy, why not celebrate a real Christian holiday this year?

Wittenberg Door Pattern

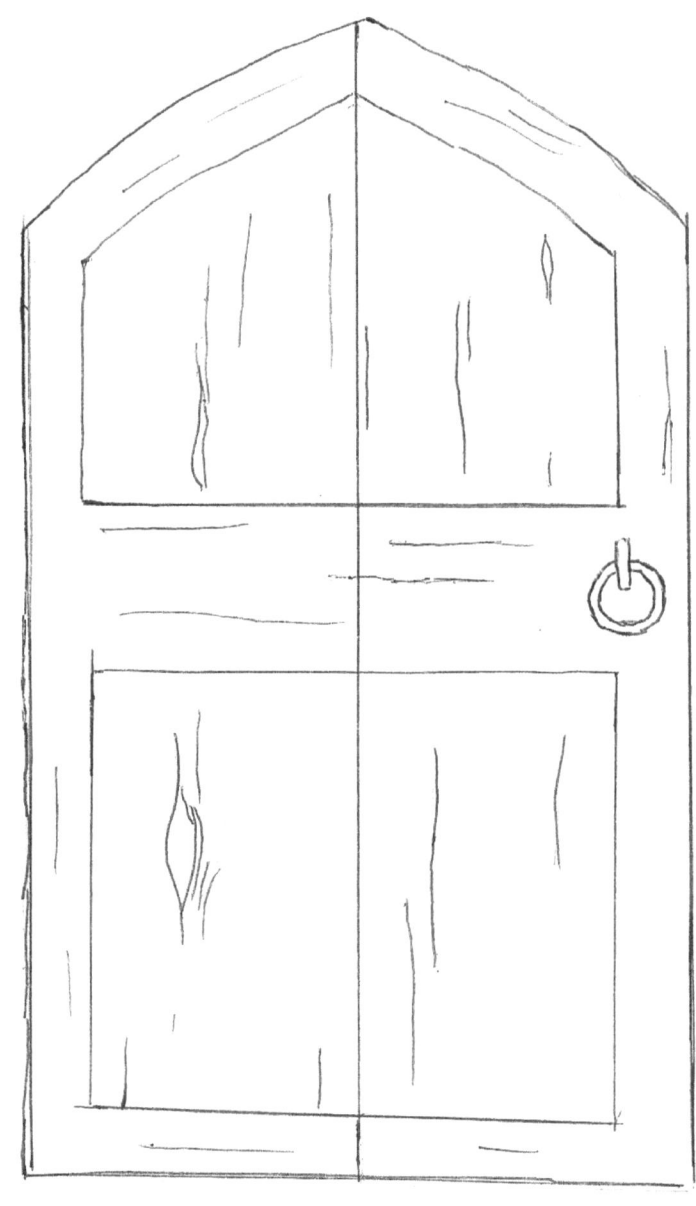

Wittenberg Door, Draw on Brown Paper if Possible (Susannah Young, Used with Permission)

"The Battle Hymn of the Reformation"

Martin Luther was more than a theologian, pastor, and student of the Bible; he was also an excellent writer and a skilled musician. One of his concerns for the newly established evangelical church was to move away from professional liturgical singing and introduce more heartfelt worship by the congregation itself.

In 1529, just a few years after the dramatic events of the Diet of Worms, Luther wrote a hymn which described Jesus Christ as the warrior prince in fulfillment of Psalm 46, blending it with a clear-eyed view of the very real dangers faced by Protestant believers of his day. We know it as "A Mighty Fortress is our God."

"Ein' feste Burg."

A mighty fortress is our God,
a bulwark never failing;
our helper He, amid the flood
of mortal ills prevailing.
    For still our ancient foe
    does seek to work us woe;
    his craft and power are great,
    and armed with cruel hate,
on earth is not his equal.

Did we in our own strength confide, our striving would be losing,
were not the right Man on our side, the Man of God's own choosing.
    You ask who that may be? Christ Jesus, it is He;
    Lord Sabaoth* His name, from age to age the same;
and He must win the battle.

*or, *Lord of Hosts*

Even though the hymn calls for courage confronting persecution, even in the face of Satan himself, there is a confident joyfulness underlying the words. In fact, Luther's original melody had a dance-like rhythm to it; it was smoothed out by Johann Sebastian Bach a century later, and the broad and regular phrases of Bach's arrangement are the melody we recognize today.

As the Reformation spread from Germany into neighboring countries, conflict broke out. Catholic monarchies fought to regain land and people lost to the Reformation, and the wars that ensued lasted for many decades. Religion and politics were thoroughly mixed in the 16th and 17th centuries, and a difference between the faith of a believer and that of his prince was often seen as an act of treason – so when Luther's hymn calls for believers to *"Let goods and kindred go-- this mortal life also,"* it was a very real danger that he himself had faced. From the very beginning, "A Mighty Fortress" has been both an encouragement for believers and in many places, a patriotic hymn as well.

English versions differ!

The first English translation, in 1539, was by Miles Coverdale, the first Englishman to translate the entire Bible. Coverdale had spent several years in the Flemish city of Antwerp and was fluent in German – in fact, many parts of his first Bible were based on Luther's prior translation! Like many early reformers, Coverdale helped adapt well-liked Lutheran hymns for the use of English churches.

The most familiar translation in American hymnbooks was prepared by Frederic H. Hedge in 1829. Just as Luther made a free adaptation from the words and ideas of Psalm 46, Hedge made a poetic translation that follows the thoughts of Luther's verses without following every word.

Surprisingly, Lutheran hymnbooks in America use different words to express the same thoughts. The first Lutheran clergyman arrived in the colonies just twenty years after the *Mayflower*, but Lutheran churches continued to use German in their worship well into the 1800s. They were divided for many decades on whether to us German or English in worship and teaching, and immigration from Germany in the early 1800's supplied a continuous flow of new German-speaking church members. In 1868, a Lutheran body in Pennsylvania published a composite version utilizing a nearly word-for-word translation of Luther's verses, and this is the foundation of the modern

Lutheran version. It is different from Hedge's translation, but the same thoughts and encouragement are expressed. Compare the two below and notice how they differ:

Hedge's familiar version	**A Lutheran version from 1918**
A mighty fortress is our God,	*A mighty fortress is our God,*
A bulwark never failing;	*A trusty Shield and Weapon;*
Our helper He, amid the flood	*He helps us free from every need*
Of mortal ills prevailing.	*That hath us now o'ertaken.*
* For still our ancient foe*	* The old bitter foe*
* Does seek to work us woe;*	* Means us deadly woe;*
* His craft and power are great,*	* Deep guile and great might*
* And armed with cruel hate,*	* Are his dread arms in fight:*
On earth is not his equal.	*On earth is not his equal.*

Fun Fact: In the 1953 movie *Martin Luther*, the closing scene shows a large congregation singing Luther's hymn in English – using the Lutheran version. The film, after all, was made by the Lutheran Production Board! But since the movie was filmed on location, the actors were all German extras, and though singing in English, their pronunciation sometimes follows German practice – like pronouncing "guile" with two syllables, "guy-la." Notice the difference in the rhythm of the interior lines, as well.

A Mighty Fortress

Lyrics: Martin Luther, 1529 - **Translation:** Frederic H. Hedge, 1829)

A mighty fortress is our God, a bulwark never failing;
Our helper He, amid the flood of mortal ills prevailing:
    For still our ancient foe
    doth seek to work us woe;
    His craft and pow'r are great,
    and, armed with cruel hate,
On earth is not his equal.

Did we in our own strength confide, our striving would be losing,
Were not the right Man on our side, the Man of God's own choosing:
    Dost ask who that may be?
    Christ Jesus, it is He;
    Lord Sabaoth, His Name,
    from age to age the same,
And He must win the battle.

And though this world, with devils filled, should threaten to undo us,
We will not fear, for God hath willed His truth to triumph through us;
    The Prince of Darkness grim,
    we tremble not for him;
    His rage we can endure,
    for lo, his doom is sure,
One little word shall fell him.

That word above all earthly pow'rs, no thanks to them, abideth;
The Spirit and the gifts are ours through Him Who with us sideth;
    Let goods and kindred go,
    this mortal life also;
    The body they may kill:
    God's truth abideth still,
His kingdom is forever!

ALL PEOPLE THAT ON EARTH DO DWELL: "OLD ONE HUNDREDTH"

Psalm 100 adapted by William Keethe (1561) – Doxology (v. 5) by Thomas Ken (1674)
Tune: Louis Bourgeois

While Luther became famous for his hymns, some churches preferred to adapt the words of the Bible more directly.

The familiar *Doxology* sung in many churches today comes from the *Anglo-Genevan Psalter,* a collection of "metrical psalms" prepared by English and Scottish refugees in Calvin's city. The tune is called "Old 100th" from its use with Psalm 100.

Psalm 100 (William Keethe, 1561)	**Psalm 100 (Geneva Bible, 1560)**
All people that on earth do dwell, sing to the Lord with cheerful voice, Him serve with fear, His praise forth tell: come ye before Him and rejoice.	1 *Sing ye loud unto the Lord, all the earth.* 2 *Serve the Lord with gladness: come before him with joyfulness.*
The Lord ye know is God indeed, without our aid He did us make: We are His flock, He doth us feed, and for His sheep He doth us take.	3 *Know ye that even the Lord is God: he hath made us, and not we ourselves: we are his people, and the sheep of his pasture.*
O enter then His gates with praise, approach with joy His courts unto: Praise, laud, and bless His Name always, for it is seemly so to do.	4 *Enter into his gates with praise, and into his courts with rejoicing: praise him and bless his Name.*
For why the Lord our God is good, His mercy is forever sure: His truth at all times firmly stood, and shall from age to age endure.	5 *For the Lord is good: his mercy is everlasting, and his truth is from generation to generation.*
Praise God from Whom all blessings flow Praise Him, all creatures here below Praise Him above, ye heavenly host Praise Father, Son, and Holy Ghost.	

Now Thank We All Our God

Lyrics: *Martin Rinckart (1586-1649)* - **Translator:** *Catherine Winkworth (1827-1878)*

Martin Rinckart was born in Saxony and lived through the Thirty Years War, a religious conflict which developed into a struggle for political dominance between the great powers of Europe. The walled town where he served as a pastor became a center for war refugees, and when starvation and epidemic broke out, Rinckart had to lead over 40 to 50 funerals *a day*. Tradition says this hymn of thanksgiving was written to celebrate the end of a siege.

Now thank we all our God, with heart and hands and voices,
    Who wondrous things has done, in Whom this world rejoices;
Who from our mothers' arms has blessed us on our way
    With countless gifts of love, and still is ours today.

O may this bounteous God through all our life be near us,
    With ever joyful hearts and blessed peace to cheer us;
And keep us in His grace, and guide us when perplexed;
    And free us from all ills, in this world and the next!

All praise and thanks to God the Father now be given;
    The Son and Him Who reigns with Them in highest Heaven;
The one eternal God, whom earth and Heaven adore;
    For thus it was, is now, and shall be evermore.

Reformation Day   Hal & Melanie Young

Who Puts His Trust in God Most Just

Lyrics: Joachim Magdeburg, 1525-1587 - **Translator:** Catherine Winkworth

Joachim Magdeburg entered the University of Wittenberg two years before the death of Luther. Changing levels of tolerance for Protestants in northern Germany kept him on the move; he was exiled twice and served at different times as a deacon, pastor, or military chaplain. This chorale is a prayer incorporating the same themes as Luther's great hymn – courage in the face of deadly opposition, trusting in God, Christ, and the Scripture!

Who puts his trust in God most just
    Hath built his house securely -- hath built his house securely;
He who relies on Jesus Christ,
    Shall reach His heav'n most surely -- shall reach His heav'n most surely;
        Then fixed on Thee, My trust shall be, For Thy truth cannot alter;
        While mine Thou art, Not death's worst smart
    Shall make my courage falter -- shall make my courage falter.

Though fiercest foes my course oppose,
    A dauntless front I'll show them -- a dauntless front I'll show them;
My Champion Thou, Lord Christ, art now,
    Who soon shalt overthrow them -- Who soon shalt overthrow them!
        And if but Thee I have in me, With Thy good gifts and Spirit,
        Nor death nor hell, I know full well,
    Shall hurt me, through Thy merit -- shall hurt me, through Thy merit.

I rest me here without a fear,
    By Thee shall all be given -- by Thee shall all be given,
That I can need, O Friend indeed,
    For this life or for heaven -- for this life or for heaven.
        O make me true, My heart renew, My soul and flesh deliver!
        Lord, hear my prayer, And in Thy care,
    Keep me in peace forever -- keep me in peace forever.

Tune: https://youtu.be/5wFmo_dApQI and https://youtu.be/UTVnllPXKQ8

Reformation Day Feast

Since the Reformation first took hold in Germany and Switzerland, we enjoy having a German or Swiss meal on Reformation Day. That used to require a lot of pre-planning since you couldn't easily find the ingredients, but now that German grocery stores like Aldi and Lidl are spreading across the country, you can find the things you need in many areas. It helps that Reformation comes at the end of the same month as Oktoberfest!

Of course, you can serve anything you like, but having a special themed meal makes occasions like this more memorable for our families – and it's just a fun thing to look forward to! Here are some possible menus:

German Sausages
Bratwurst and/or Knockwurst
Sauerkraut
Grandma's Green Beans
Himmel und Erde or Hot German Potato Salad
Homemade Applesauce

Swiss Fondue
Cheese Fondue or Fondue Bourguignonne
Crusty Bread
Roasted or Boiled Potatoes
Roasted Asparagus

Swiss Raclette
Raclette and Other Sliced Cheeses
Sliced Sausages, if desired
Crusty Thin-sliced Bread
New Potatoes or Sliced Boiled Potatoes
Bell Peppers & Sweet Onions
Roasted Asparagus

Cooking these things is much easier and faster with the right equipment – an Instant Pot™, a fondue pot, and/or a raclette grill. Go to our Reformation Day Resources page for recommendations: www.RaisingRealMen.com/reformation.

Germanic food culture includes a lot of potatoes and apples. Asparagus is so popular that when the new crop is available, restaurants announce the happy event with table tents!

For drinks, we serve either Spezi or Apple Cider. We learned about Spezi when we were traveling in Germany as young marrieds on a tight budget. On every *Speisekarte*, or menu, the most inexpensive soft drink listed was always Spezi, so of course, we had to try it. Oddly, it is a half and half mixture of an orange-flavored soft drink, such as Orange Crush™ or Fanta™, and a cola, such as Coke™ or Pepsi™. Don't write it off too soon! It is way better than it sounds and our family has actually become quite fond of it. There's an article about it on Wikipedia - https://en.wikipedia.org/wiki/Spezi

Apple cider or juice, called *Apfelsaft*, is another common drink in throughout the region.

Because we play games with candy for rewards, we usually don't do a dessert on Reformation Day. We have plenty of sweets!

Bratwurst with Sauerkraut

Knockwurst or other German sausages may be cooked the same way.

Bratwurst, fresh, pre-cooked, or frozen, two or more per person.

1 t. Beef Base in 1 cup water (optional, but see below) or a cup of beef broth

1-2 cans or jars of Sauerkraut (optional, but see discussion below)

Sausages may be cooked on the stove, on the grill, or in the Instant Pot™

On the Stove

If frozen, first defrost in the fridge or microwave. Place bratwurst in single layer in an oiled skillet that has a lid. Saute until nicely browned. Carefully add about one-half to one cup of beef broth or water (plus beef base and sauerkraut, if desired) and cover with lid. Cook until thoroughly heated (if pre-cooked) or cooked through (if raw).

On the Grill

To cook on the grill, if frozen first defrost in the fridge or microwave. Cook raw bratwurst over medium heat, turning frequently for about 20-25 minutes or until cooked through. Cook pre-cooked bratwurst over medium heat, turning frequently until piping hot through.

In the Instant Pot™

There is no need to thaw your bratwurst. If you like your bratwurst browned (and it's nicer that way, but not essential if you are in a hurry), turn the Instant Pot to Sauté, add a thin layer of oil, and brown the sausages a single layer at a time. Add a cup of beef broth or water with ½ to 1 teaspoon of beef base stirred in. Add sauerkraut, if desired (see sauerkraut notes below). Cook on Manual on High for the time listed below:

Pre-Cooked Bratwurst, 6 minutes

Raw Bratwurst, 8 minutes

Frozen, Pre-Cooked Bratwurst, 8 minutes

Frozen, Raw Bratwurst, 10 minutes

Sauerkraut Notes

Sauerkraut is something you tend to either love or hate, but it is possible to learn to love it. Sauerkraut is a fermented food that has vitamins C and K and fiber, too. If your family isn't fond of sauerkraut, try draining the liquid from it and cooking it in beef broth (or water with beef base added). If it's still too strong, rinse it after you drain it next time. Some varieties of sauerkraut are milder than others, as well. Bavarian sauerkraut tends to be milder and sweeter and often has caraway seed added.

What is Beef Base?

Beef base is super-concentrated beef stock. It's a paste that you can buy in a tub or jar at any grocery store. It has a much better flavor than the typical bouillon cube.

Hot German Potato Salad

*We cook as much of this as we can fit in the pot. You can't have too much!
It's good reheated or even cold.*

6 medium potatoes, sliced in rounds 1/4 to 1/3 inch thick, with skins preferably

6 strips bacon

1 medium onion

1/2 cup vinegar, white or cider

1/4 cup water

1 t. sugar

1/8 t. dry mustard OR 1 t. prepared mustard

1/8 t. paprika (optional)

1 t. pickle relish OR one dill pickle, diced

Boil potatoes until done, but still firm. Meanwhile, fry bacon in *large* frying pan. Remove bacon and pour off all but two or three tablespoons of fat. Chop onions and sauté them in the bacon grease. Add the rest of the ingredients, except for potatoes, to the pan. Break up the bacon and return to pan, as well. Drain potatoes. Bring vinegar mixture to a boil, add the potato slices, and gently mix. Serve hot or cold. Great with sausages, hamburgers, schnitzel, or veal cutlets.

Himmel und Erde

This traditional German side dish is called Heaven and Earth because it contains apples and potatoes. Although Himmel und Erde *and Hot German Potato Salad appear similar, they are quite different!*

6-8 medium potatoes, diced, or 10-12 new potatoes, chunked

3-4 apples, tart apples are best, peeled, cored, and sliced or chunked

1 onion

5 strips bacon

Pinch nutmeg

Sugar or honey, about a tablespoon

Butter, 2-4 tablespoons

Place apples and potatoes in a stockpot, cover with water and boil until tender. Drain.

Or, place apples and potatoes in the Instant Pot™ with 1/2 or 3/4 cup of water. Set on Manual, High, for 7 minutes. Do a quick release. Drain any remaining water.

While potatoes and apples are cooking, fry bacon. Drain on paper towels and crumble. Sauté onions in bacon grease. Drain.

At this point, you can mash potatoes and apples together with a potato masher, mixer, or blender. Alternately, you can leave the apples and potatoes in chunks for texture. We prefer it in chunks.

Add butter and sugar to potatoes and apples and place in serving bowl. Sprinkle with nutmeg. Distribute onions and bacon on top. Serve with sausages or other main dish.

Grandma's Green Beans

An Instant Pot™ recipe that reminds us of the green beans Hal's grandmother home-canned.

1 1/2 pounds fresh green beans, washed and snapped

1 cup water

1 teaspoon beef base (or beef stock instead of water and beef base)

1 slice bacon

4-5 sliced mushrooms (optional)

1 teaspoon minced garlic

1/2 teaspoon salt

Dash of pepper

Set Instant Pot™ to Sauté and fry bacon in it until it renders (releases its fat). Add the rest of the ingredients. Cook at Manual on High for 15 minutes and quick release pressure. Delicious! Tastes like Grandma's!

Cheese Fondue

A classic peasant's dish that has become an elegant party meal!

1 clove garlic

2 cups liquid for base, traditionally a dry white wine such as a Sauvignon Blanc, which is the easiest to use. White grape or apple cider can be used to avoid alcohol, but it is a little more difficult to make it turn out and 1/4 cup of lemon juice should be added for acidity. Although the alcohol mostly cooks out, sometimes children appreciate the sweeter juice-based fondue. Generally, we make a pot of each.

2 pounds cheese, or 8 cups grated, traditionally a mixture of Gruyere and Emmentaler (Swiss cheese actually from Switzerland). You can use any hard, full fat cheese. Although we prefer Gruyere and Emmentaler, we often use the less expensive ordinary Swiss cheese.

1/4 cup kirsch (cherry brandy) is traditional, but we don't use it ourselves

4 T. cornstarch

Pinch nutmeg

Crusty French bread, cubed (read instructions)

Cube the bread. Letting it get a bit stale while you cook won't hurt it, in fact, it helps. Cut cubes 1-2 inches, making sure every piece has crust on one side.

Cut the garlic in half and rub the cut side around the inside of the pan.

Grate the cheese. Sprinkle the cornstarch over the cheese and toss to coat.

Add wine or cider to the pot and set it on the stove on medium (or slightly higher for cider). Warm up the liquid until it is just on the edge of boiling.

Add the cheese (coated in cornstarch) by small handfuls, stirring in a figure eight motion until it is ENTIRELY MELTED and mixed in before you add more. At first, the strands of cheese will turn into tiny bits, then you can add more. It's important not to add more cheese too early. This takes time, but rushing at this point will leave you with stringy clumped cheese in the bottom of cloudy wine. Don't hurry!

While you are cooking the fondue, have someone else set the table with saucers or small plates, pour drinks, and place the bread cubes in a basket or several baskets or bowls around the table.

When all the cheese has been added and it has thickened nicely, add the kirsch, if desired, sprinkle nutmeg on top, and take to the table.

You will need a way to keep it hot at the table. If you are using a fondue pot, there will be an electric heating element or a place to put a lighted Sterno™ can. Some older instant pots will use an alcohol burner and you will need to buy denatured alcohol. If you don't have a fondue pot, see our list of great resources at www.RaisingRealMen.com/reformation. If you can't afford one right now, in a pinch you can use a crockpot with a way to adjust the temperature or a hot plate with a regular pot on it.

You will also need long fondue forks in order for everyone to be able to reach into the pot.

Once the fondue is on the table, call your family to the table, give thanks and begin!

Pick up a cube of bread and put it on a fondue fork with the crust side at the bottom of the fork. As you dip your bread in the cheese, stir the cheese with it and wipe it along the inside edge of the pot so the cheese doesn't stick.

If you lose your bread in the pot, you are supposed to kiss the Swiss Miss (or Mister!) to your right.

It's wise to alternate bigger and smaller children so the older children can dip for the younger ones who may not be able to safely reach.

You can serve this alone with just saucers for plates or with asparagus, green beans, or salad. Winter fruits like orange slices or grapefruits make a delicious finish to the meal. This is a classic winter peasant's meal in Switzerland.

Raclette

A cheese-lover's paradise and a whole lot of fun!

Several ounces of cheese per person. Use hard or semi-hard cheeses like Raclette, Swiss, Cheddar, Provolone, Gruyere, or others.

Several ounces of sliced ready to eat sausages per person, such as smoked sausage, kielbasa, bratwurst, andouille, or knockwurst.

Sliced sweet onions, bell peppers, and/or mushrooms.

Boiled or roasted potatoes. New potatoes, red potatoes, or Yukon potatoes are wonderful. Slice larger potatoes.

Crusty bread, sliced thinly.

Butter, as needed.

Pepper and peppermill, if desired.

Place all ingredients in an attractive arrangement on platters. Keep sausages separate from other ingredients.

Set the table with drinks, raclette spatulas, small or salad plates or saucers, forks, and napkins. Heat up the raclette grill.

Each diner should select a type of cheese to place in their small pan under the broiler.

They can then select vegetables and sausage to cook on top of the grill, adding butter as needed for it to sauté nicely.

While all of this is cooking, diners should choose bread or potato for their plate. When the cheese is melted and beginning to brown, the diner should use the spatula to slide the cheese onto the bread or potato. Use a peppermill to add a little spice, if desired.

The wonderful thing about this meal is that it is interactive and time-consuming. This encourages a lively conversation and celebratory spirit! Just having raclette to eat will go a long way to make your party a success.

Fondue Bourguignonne

Although named after a province in France, this dish originated in Switzerland.

Oil, enough to fill your fondue pot halfway (use an oil that doesn't smoke easily, such as canola, sunflower, or peanut oil)

Beef, enough to feed your family (a cut which is tender enough to serve as steak is best). Some versions use chicken as well, but beef is a little safer to handle raw at the table.

Cube the steak in bite-size pieces. Set it out at room temperature for about an hour.

Warm the oil in the fondue pot until it is hot enough to cook a bread cube golden brown in 30-45 seconds.

While the oil is warming, finish setting the table and getting any side dishes to the table.

Call everyone to the table and discuss safety. It's important that the table is sturdy and that it not be jostled. Children should not put their own meat in the oil or remove it.

Stick a long fondue fork into the meat so that the tines protrude from the other side. Place the meat (still attached to the fork) into the hot oil. Leave until done to your taste. Use another fork to remove the steak from the fondue fork. Do NOT stick the hot fork in your mouth. It WILL burn you.

When Melanie was a child, her family served this with small bowls of dips set at each plate. We love ours with *Marchand du Vin* sauce and perhaps a horseradish sauce. Asparagus and a potato dish are delicious with this.

Do NOT attempt this if your children can not be trusted to sit quietly and obey commands. It is hot oil, after all. We also would not recommend using a makeshift fondue pot substitute for this recipe. See our Reformation Day Resources at www.RaisingRealMen.com/reformation for recommendations.

Marchand du Vin Sauce

This is absolutely incredible with Fondue Bourguignonne or on any steak.

1 cup of sliced mushrooms. We love baby portabellas, but white mushrooms are delicious, too.

1/2 stick of real butter (4 T.)

4 T. flour

1/4 cup of sherry or red wine (cooking wine from the grocery store is acceptable)

1 3/4 cups of strong beef broth, or 1 3/4 cups of water and 1 1/2 t. beef base

Melt the butter in a skillet until bubbly, but not at all browned. Sauté the mushrooms until soft. If you are unaccustomed to making a roux, you might temporarily remove the mushrooms at this point. Add the flour and stir into the butter. Add more butter if necessary to make a loose, soft paste. If it is at all clumpy, add more butter! Stir and sauté until the roux (flour and butter mixture) changes texture slightly and begins looking a little cooked or bready. It's hard to describe, but if you watch carefully, you will see the change just as it starts becoming very slightly golden.

Add the wine to deglaze the pan, scraping up all the delicious little bits off the bottom. Add the broth slowly, stirring well with each addition so it doesn't get lumpy. Return the mushrooms to the pan if you removed them. Simmer until the sauce thickens and serve with any beef dish. This is so incredibly delicious!

Roasted Asparagus

This vegetable is wildly popular in Germany, with Germans eating asparagus every day during what they call the Spargelzeit season, when it's available fresh.

1 bundle asparagus, washed and trimmed, Germans prefer the white variety, but that is harder to find in America, so you may need to use the green.

Olive oil

Minced garlic

Salt & pepper

Parmesan cheese (optional)

Preheat oven to 425 degrees. Trim the woody ends off the asparagus. Lay out in a single layer on a cookie sheet. Drizzle with olive oil and sprinkle with garlic, salt and pepper, and parmesan, if you wish.

Roast at 425 degrees until done to your liking. This could be anywhere from 8 to 15 minutes. It's hard to be more exact because asparagus varies so widely in diameter and some people like it crunchy and others soft. You're just going to have to keep an eye on it.

INSTANT POT™ APPLE SAUCE

Although you can cook this on the stovetop, the Instant Pot™ takes all the stirring and watching away.

3 pounds of apples, a tasty variety like Gala, Fuji, McIntosh, or a mixture.

1/2 cup water

1/2 tsp. cinnamon

Pinch nutmeg

Pinch mace

1/4 cup, more or less to taste, sugar, honey, maple syrup, or other sweetener, or none at all, if you prefer.

Peel, core, and chunk apples. By far the easiest way to do this is to use a spiral apple slicer. We've had one for years and our kids love to use it – it's fast and easy. Our recommendations can be found at our Resource page here: www.RaisingRealMen.com/Reformation.

Put apples and water in Instant Pot™ and seal. Set on Manual, high, for 10 minutes. When it beeps, allow it to naturally release pressure for 5 minutes, then release. Add sweetener and spices to taste. Serve hot or cold. Delicious!

What About the Other Holiday?

Readers often ask us, "Do you guys celebrate Halloween?" We had a lot of discussion about this when we were first married. We went back and forth between the fun we'd had as kids and the opportunity to perhaps share the gospel with neighbors who came to the door, and our discomfort with the whole celebration of gruesomeness which Halloween was becoming.

Many Christians we know find themselves torn, too.

Our friends who do celebrate Halloween tell us, "It's just pretend. Ease up!" and "I give the neighbor kids really good candy and tracts." Lately we're hearing, "It's a day to mock the devil and death. It celebrates that they have no power over us." We're not convinced.

Although the Lord can use a tract handed out at Halloween, we think it's more likely to cause resentment than repentance in unbelievers. That sort of evangelism isn't in any sort of relationship context, and it's not really appropriate to the situation. When we build a relationship with those around us, they can see our love and concern for them and know we're not trying to add a scalp to our church belt. They know us enough to understand we're sharing the most important thing in the world with them.

We'd rather lift up Christ than put down His enemy. Though we appreciate the boldness of our friends that say they are mocking the devil on Halloween, Luke 10:20 tells us, *"Nevertheless, do not rejoice in this, that the spirits are subject to you, but rejoice that your names are written in heaven."* It doesn't seem like "mocking the devil" is what we're supposed to be doing.

Besides, the world doesn't seem to be mocking these things as much as reveling in them. Demons, horrors, and death are not something to celebrate. Our Savior suffered and died to conquer these things.

But, isn't it all just pretend? Throughout Scripture, "just pretend" doesn't cut it. It's about our heart as much as our actions. Proverbs 26:18-19 says, *"Like a madman who throws firebrands, arrows, and death is the man who deceives his neighbor and says, "I am only joking!"* In the New Testament, the Lord assures us that merely looking at a woman lustfully is committing adultery in your heart, and hating your brother makes you a murderer at heart. We don't think you should play at sin.

And sin seems to be more and more involved. It's not the same holiday we remember from childhood. Increasingly, it's an adult holiday, representing over $9 billion spent in the United States each Halloween, and costumes are getting more and more troubling.

Although we don't have any problem at all with costumes, the usual Halloween costume tradition communicates a couple of ideas which are polar opposites and both wrong.

The first idea is that there's nothing to the idea of demons, witches, and all the monstrosities we associate with the holiday. They are all superstition and ghost stories, people say. Nothing more than play-acting at Halloween, all just good clean fun.

There's a problem with that. Even if it's true that it's all just a game, people are not just assuming the fantastic shapes of Frankensteins and werewolves of old black-and-white movies. They're dressing in too-realistic fashion as victims of domestic violence, survivors of gruesome accidents, and criminals of all sorts. Even worse yet are the sensual fantasies, inappropriate teases that are immodest and immoral in nature, or sexualizing small children. You can't let the kids look at costume catalogs!

Even if the things of horror are not real, there are people who think they are. Joe Leaphorn, the Navaho police detective featured in Tony Hillerman's mystery stories, often encounters stories of "skin-walkers," the shape-shifting witches of Navaho legend. Leaphorn says in one of the early novels, "I don't believe in skin-walkers, but I believe in people who do." What he meant was it's immaterial whether such things exist or not when there are real people who *do* believe in them and because of that belief, do things which have a real impact on those around them.

Missionaries encounter this all the time. Whether the local witch doctor or shaman has real spiritual power or not is somewhat beside the point; if the local people believe he has power, they fear him and defer to his will. The missionary must overcome the social power this figure wields in order to free the people to follow Christ—the *real* spiritual power.

On the other hand, we shouldn't make light of real tragedy and real sin—don't sugar coat it—as if it's all a game. R.C. Sproul Jr. observed that erecting toy tombstones in your yard isn't a laughing matter; death is real, and for many of us and our neighbors, death is a very, very bad prospect. It's not a joke.

The second idea is that ghoulies and ghosties *are* real, but it's okay to pretend about them.

The Bible sort of squelches that for us. Consider that when God established His people in a formal way, in the national identity of Israel, He explicitly told them to stay away from that stuff and the people that practice it:

There shall not be found among you ... anyone who practices divination or tells fortunes or interprets omens, or a sorcerer, or a charmer or a medium or a necromancer or one who inquires of the dead, for whoever does these things is an abomination to the Lord. (Deuteronomy 18:10-12 ESV)

In fact, He made it a capital offense to follow these teachings (Leviticus 20:27) or consult with those who do (Leviticus 20:6). It's one of the reasons He wiped out the ancient Canaanites and gave their land to the Jews.

It's interesting that He doesn't suggest that these people are truly powerful—He simply says we must avoid it all. For them (and us), it's a betrayal, seeking after forbidden spirituality when you've already met the source of true spiritual power, no different than seeking a physical relationship outside of your marriage—except this time you're cheating on God, and you can't sneak around on Him.

It kind of takes the fun out of seances and Ouija boards.

The other option is that spiritual things are real, both good and bad. And if you believe the Bible and believe what Jesus Himself said, you have to take that as given.

Are there bad spirits in every tree and stone beside the road? We don't see any evidence of it in Scripture or nature. But it's plain that besides the evil that men do, there *are* spiritual forces, even personal ones, which we need to take seriously. Jesus wasn't playing make believe or joshing along the cultural superstitions when He confronted demons: there are many incidents in the Gospels where Jesus displayed His power over them, casting out unclean spirits which had oppressed individuals a variety of ways (check out Matthew chapters 8, 9, 12, 15, and 17; Mark 1, 5, 7 and 9; and Luke 4, 8, 9, and 11, for a start.)

Jesus never backed away from correcting misunderstandings and human additions to God's word, even in the face of mob violence and physical threat to Himself, but He never "corrects" the "mythological" view that evil spirits are at work in some people's lives. Instead, He defeats them, then teaches His people to understand their nature and how to combat them. He took it seriously, as did the apostles.

If we believe the Bible, and we believe Jesus, then we need to believe that whatever nonsense and mythologies humans may have created in addition to the truth, there is a fundamental reality—there are beings and powers we need to be aware of and avoid, not toy with. Christ has overcome them on earth, and God overrules them throughout the universe, but we need to keep away from them.

And for that reason, well, let's just say we don't get into the spirit of Halloween. Join us in celebrating a solid Christian tradition instead.

Happy Reformation Day!

OTHER HOLIDAY RESOURCES

Thanksgiving was meant to be about more than pigging out and pigskins. Here's all you need to host your own celebration for the extended family that honors God instead of just football, much as we love it. Teach your kids the true stories of Thanksgiving and learn how to teach them real gratitude, too.

Contains primary historical sources, activity ideas, cooking tips and schedules, secret family recipes, song sheets, and ideas for making this holiday more Christ-centered than ever.

When Thanksgiving is over, you can make the rest of the holiday season better, too!

Many Christians we know are so tired of the commercialization of Christmas that they are ready to throw out the whole thing, but why not use our culture's preoccupation with the holidays to tell the real story of God's incarnation to our children, our families, and our neighbors? This book will inspire you take the gospel to your community with carols, will help you to direct your kid's attention away from getting, getting, getting toward giving and blessing, and give you lots of ideas of how to make the holiday season more fun and more Christ-centered.

Find both books and many other resources to help you make Biblical family life practical at www.RaisingRealMen.com.

www.ingramcontent.com/pod-product-compliance
Lightning Source LLC
Chambersburg PA
CBHW050756110526
44588CB00002B/17